THIS BOOK BELONGS TO:

_____

DESERT TORTOISE

RATTLE SNAKE

ALLIGATOR

HERON

CRAB

ORCA WHALE

EMPEROR PENGUIN

PORCUPINE

RACCOON

WOODPECKER

TOUCAN

ANTEATER

Please consider leaving a review of our book on Amazon.
We'd appreciate it very much!

Thank you!
The happy crayons team

And if you're looking for more to color, please visit:
happycrayons.com

Copyright © 2021 by Simple Future LLC.
All rights reserved.

ISBN: 978-1-7368948-2-8

No part of this publication may be reproduced, distributed, or transmitted in any form or by any means, including photocopying, recording, or other electronic or mechanical methods, without the prior written permission of the publisher, except in the case of brief quotations for the purposes of book reviews.

Made in United States
Orlando, FL
11 March 2022